football's new wave

Jevon Kearse

Force of One

BY
MARK STEWART

THE MILLBROOK PRESS
BROOKFIELD, CONNECTICUT

M

THE MILLBROOK PRESS

Produced by
BITTERSWEET PUBLISHING
John Sammis, President
and
TEAM STEWART, INC.
RESEARCHED AND EDITED BY MIKE KENNEDY

Series Design and Electronic Page Makeup by
JAFFE ENTERPRISES
Ron Jaffe

All photos courtesy AP/ Wide World Photos, Inc., except the following:
SportsChrome USA: Rob Tringali Jr., photographer — Cover
Fort Myers News Press — Pages 6, 7
Wade Hummell — Page 8
The following images are from the collection of Team Stewart:
NFL Properties, Inc. (© 1993) — Page 15
T.C.G. (© 1970) — Page 37
NFL Properties, Inc. (© 2000) — Page 44

Printed in the United States of America

Published by
The Millbrook Press, Inc.
2 Old New Milford Road
Brookfield, Connecticut   06804

www.millbrookpress.com

Library of Congress Cataloging-in-Publication Data

Stewart, Mark.
    Jevon Kearse : force of one / by Mark Stewart.
      p. cm. — (Football's new wave)
    Includes index.
    ISBN 0-7613-2269-8 (lib. bdg.)
    1. Kearse, Jevon, 1976—Juvenile literature. 2. Football players—United States—
Biography—Juvenile literature. [1. Kearse, Jevon, 1976– 2. Football players. 3. African
Americans—Biography.] I. Title. II. Series.
GV939.K33 S84 2001
796.332'092--dc21
[B]
                                                                          00-069550

1 3 5 7 9 10 8 6 4 2

Contents

Rising above the Pain

"There was something deep in my heart. I wanted to be better than the next person in everything."

— **JEVON KEARSE**

Kids can face a lot of pressure in their lives. There is the pressure to do well in school. There is the pressure to do well in sports. And there is the pressure to live up to the expectations of family and friends. For some, the pressure to rise above a challenging situation is greatest of all. Usually, this means overcoming obstacles in order to fulfill your potential. In the case of Jevon Kearse, the hurdles were much higher and the stakes much greater.

Jevon was born on September 3, 1976, in Fort Myers, a city of 50,000 people in southwest Florida. His father's name was Joseph, but he never met his father. Shortly before Jevon was born, Joseph Kearse was murdered. As he grew up, Jevon got to know his dad through the stories of others. In these stories, he seemed larger than life. He was an enormous man with a talent for singing, and he was a terrific athlete. Ignoring these gifts, Joseph instead chose a life of crime. He was so big and scary that he was able to

Jevon Kearse's dad died before Jevon was born.
It turns out they had much in common—size, athletic talent,
intelligence—but Jevon found a way to make the most of his abilities.

A graduation photo of Jevon and his best friend, Cisco Navas, is proudly displayed by Cisco's mother, Yolanda.

commit robberies without a weapon. Even the Fort Myers police were frightened of him.

After Joe was killed, the police continued to be involved with Jevon's family. When Jevon was just two years old, his 57-year-old grandfather, George Kearse, was killed in a gun battle outside his home. A few months later, Jevon's cousin, Danny, was shot and killed in self-defense when he attacked someone. Another cousin, Marcell, went to jail for attempted murder when Jevon was little; he died in a prison hospital a few years ago. "I had to grow up fast," Jevon says. "I had a lot of obstacles to overcome. It made me a lot stronger, growing up like that."

Focusing on his own future enabled Jevon to survive his violent childhood. The more he concentrated on how he wanted his life to be, the happier he became. And the happier Jevon was, the easier it was to deal with the pain and confusion of day-to-day life. This meant staying out of trouble, and following a path that would help him rise above his surroundings. He found this path between the covers of his schoolbooks. "I took it on myself to stay in my books and make something of myself," Jevon says.

There *was* happiness in Jevon's early life. He fondly remembers fishing with his grandmother, Lucille. "She'd sit there in her long chair with a cane pole in her hand and tobacco in her cheek, and I'm telling you she was the queen!" he laughs. "Every so often she'd catch a mullet and say, 'Y'all take this fish for me and put another worm on there.' All she'd do was pull 'em out of the water, and I'd do the rest."

These lazy days outdoors were a relief from the cramped apartment in the Sabal Arms housing project, where Jevon and his six brothers and sisters lived. Jevon was

Lessie Mae's second child. He was closest to his older brother, J. J. (short for Joseph, Jr.), and his younger half brother, Jermaine. The three caught crabs, staged wrestling matches, and played football. They were all tall, fast, and extremely coordinated.

As the boys got older, J. J. began hanging around a rough crowd. Jevon did not like his brother's friends, and decided to steer clear of them. Instead, Jevon got his thrills on the football field, where he was the star of the Lee Middle School team. Jevon's coaches remember him at this age as a player who could not be stopped when the action got fast and furious. His teachers remember him as a very good student, although he was shy about speaking in class. Like his father, Jevon stuttered when he got nervous.

Jevon's friends and family knew him as a kind, gentle young man. Even on the football field, he rarely tackled people as hard as he could. You really had to do something mean to get him angry. A boy named Cisco Navas learned this in eighth grade, when he tried to steal Jevon's milk carton at lunch. Jevon and Cisco (also a big kid) grappled furiously until Jevon slammed him to the ground. After the two were separated, they were sent to the principal's office. While they waited, the boys agreed to say they were just pretending. They convinced the principal not to punish them, and from that day on they were best friends.

The more time Jevon spent with Cisco and his family, the more he realized how awful his own home life was. Cisco and his mother (a widow) lived in a

No one can ever wear Jevon's #25 for the Knights again—the school retired his number.

Jevon and high-school coach Wade Hummell. Unlike most players his age, the bigger Jevon grew, the quicker he got.

house in less-crowded North Fort Myers. Their property was surrounded by 6 acres (2.4 hectares) of wooded land, where the two boys explored and played, and just talked. It was a calm and peaceful place, unlike any Jevon had ever known. In the fall of 1992, right around Jevon's 16th birthday, he moved in with Cisco. Leaving his family was not easy, but the more he thought about it, the more sense it made. It took him away from the mean streets of the Dunbar section of Fort Myers. "And it was good for my mom," Jevon points out. "It was one less mouth to feed."

The move north had a positive effect on Jevon's schoolwork, too. In the projects, there were too many distractions—and the apartment was too noisy and crowded to do homework and study for tests. At Cisco's house, *nothing* happened until the boys had completed at least an hour of homework, reading, or studying. Cisco's mother saw to that. Jevon's grades shot up immediately.

So did Jevon. He was now one of the tallest kids in school. And because of the weight-gaining supplements he and Cisco gulped down each day, Jevon was also one of the most muscular. The amazing thing about Jevon was that, no matter how big he became, he seemed to get more athletic. Usually, when teenagers grow inches at a time and pack on extra pounds, they get slower or their coordination suffers. With Jevon, it was just the opposite.

In 1993, he and Cisco transferred to North Fort Myers High School. Jevon became the Red Knights' strong safety and tight end—making crunching tackles on defense and delivering steamroller blocks on offense. Jevon was particularly good on special teams. When the Red Knights kicked off, opponents would search for where he was playing and then run away from him. This rarely made a difference, because he was the fastest tackler on the field. When other teams kicked off, they aimed the ball away from

Did You Know?

Jevon has two great role models to look up to—Deacon Jones and Warren Sapp. Jones, who played his high-school ball in Orlando, is the greatest pass rusher ever to come out of Florida. He actually invented the term "sack" when he starred for the Rams in the 1960s. Sapp, another Orlando native, was the man who beat out Jevon for Defensive Player of the Year honors in 1999.

"I've never discussed him with my mom. It would probably stir up a lot of extra stress."
JEVON ON HIS FATHER, JOSEPH KEARSE

Jevon. No one wanted to tackle him one-on-one, and often no one could. Four times, he returned kicks for touchdowns.

Jevon found joy in football that rarely came to him in the rest of his life. And although things have improved greatly since his school days, he still has the same attitude. "I just thrive on trying to be the strongest, the fastest, the quickest player on the field all the time," he explains.

High-school football is a big deal in Florida, and the Red Knights were something special. It was not unusual for 15,000 or more people to attend their games. Jevon was the star attraction, along with Cisco and a couple of other talented players, Otis Marchman and Joe Lewis. They called themselves "The Four Horsemen" and they ran roughshod over opponents. In his senior year, Jevon made 96 solo tackles, intercepted 6 passes, blocked 4 punts, and caught 24 passes for 453 yards. *USA Today* and *Super Prep* honored him as an All-American; he was also named his district's Most Valuable Player and Defensive Player of the Year.

Jevon scored in the classroom, too. By his senior year, he had a 3.6 grade-point average, and was a member of the National Honor Society. Of all the compliments paid to Jevon in high school, the words of principal Ed Stickles made him proudest. "When I look at Jevon, I see the total package," Stickles once said. "That's what gives me the biggest smile."

Go Get 'Em, Gator

chapter 1

"He didn't know how good he could be."
— COLLEGE TEAMMATE
MIKE PETERSON

With his size, skills, and grades, Jevon Kearse was the envy of every college football coach. Although the teams recruiting him differed in their opinion of where he should play, they all agreed that he would make a big impact. After carefully considering offers from around the country, Jevon narrowed his choices to five universities: Florida, Florida State, Miami, Notre Dame, and Ohio State. Each had a great football team, and each offered him the academic challenges he sought.

Deciding that he preferred snow-free winters, Jevon eventually chose the University of Florida, in Gainesville. Of the three Florida schools it seemed the most like home. It did not hurt that a cousin, Johnnie Church, was a defensive lineman for the Gators.

Jevon arrived on campus in the summer of 1995. He was listed as a safety, but as soon as the coaching staff saw him they moved him closer to the line of scrimmage. Jevon had grown to 6 feet 5 inches (196 cm) and now weighed well over 200 pounds (91 kilograms). He had the quickness to play linebacker, but also the size to be a pass rusher. Head coach Steve

Did You Know?

In college, Jevon could run the 40-yard dash in full pads in less than 4.5 seconds.

Recruiting Jevon Kearse was one of the happiest moments in Steve Spurrier's career.

Spurrier decided that the best strategy was to redshirt Jevon so he could sit out a season and learn what each position demanded.

As always, Jevon worked hard on and off the field. He was so busy getting used to college—and college football—that he never really stopped to figure out how good he was. His teammates knew. They faced him every day in practice and were in awe of his power and speed. They would laugh privately at the thought of what he would do to opponents when Coach Spurrier set him loose in 1996.

Those plans were nearly derailed that fall when Jevon was arrested. He was washing his car at a service station when a group of police officers, guns at the ready, rolled up and handcuffed him. He was taken into custody on charges of automobile theft. Jevon sat in his cell and tried to sort out this strange situation; he had never stolen a candy bar, much less a car. Soon he figured out what had happened. That summer, his brother J. J. had been caught driving a stolen vehicle in Sarasota. J. J. told the police he was Jevon, and gave them Jevon's social security number. When J. J. failed to show up for his trial, a warrant was issued for *Jevon's* arrest.

Jevon explained this case of mistaken identity to the authorities, and fortunately they believed him. By the time the law caught up with J. J., he had also been charged with armed robbery. He began serving a seven-and-a-half-year jail term in the DeSoto Correctional Institute in 1996. "I've learned what *not* to do from watching him," says Jevon sadly.

Aside from his night behind bars, Jevon's first year in college was a good one. He practiced his new positions during the week and on Saturdays watched games from the sidelines. The Florida football team had its best year ever, winning the Southeast Conference (SEC) crown for the third straight season and making it all the way to the

Jacquez Green finishes off a 96-yard touchdown catch against Northern Illinois in a 1995 game. Green was one of three great receivers on the Florida Gators.

national championship game against the Nebraska Cornhuskers. Jevon kept working that spring and summer, and by the fall of 1996 he was ready to become a star.

In truth, the 1996 Florida Gators probably could have reached the title game again without Jevon. The team was one of the best college units ever assembled. Quarterback Danny Wuerffel was the highest-rated passer in college history in 1995, and in 1996 he had his choice of big-play receivers in Ike Hilliard, Jacquez Green, and Reidel Anthony. When a running play was called, Wuerffel could choose from a group of excellent backs, including future NFL star Fred Taylor.

Bob Stoops turned Jevon into a defensive terror. Stoops went on to coach Oklahoma to a national title.

On defense, the Gators had a new look thanks to Bob Stoops, who had been Defensive Coordinator for Kansas State the year before, when the Wild Cats finished with the nation's stingiest defense. Now Stoops was a member of Spurrier's coaching staff. Florida's pass defense was its strength. Its weak spot was at linebacker and on the line, where a total of four starters, including All-American Kevin Carter, had graduated. Jevon was one of the young players expected to step up and fill these roles.

By this time, people were starting to call Jevon the "Freak." They meant it in a good way. Everyone was amazed at how a kid that big could have such great skills. With his arms outstretched, he measured 86 inches (218 cm) from the tip of one middle finger to the tip of the other—that's more than 7 feet! When he spread his hands, his thumb and pinkie were a foot apart. He had a better combination of speed and leaping ability than any of the Gators' running backs and receivers, yet he could also pump iron with the 300-pound (136-kilogram) offensive linemen.

In his first game in a Gator uniform, Jevon was sensational. The Gators, playing at home in Florida Field (nicknamed "The Swamp"), destroyed Southwest Louisiana 55–21 in front of 85,000 fans. On each of Jevon's six tackles, he could feel the cheers cascade down from the stands. When he sacked the quarterback, the crowd's roar was deafening. That day he knew he had chosen the right place to play.

Fred Taylor dives for the goal line in the national championship game against Florida State. Taylor went on to star for the NFL's Jacksonville Jaguars.

As far as the right *position* for Jevon, well, that was still up in the air. Coach Stoops used him differently in different situations. Sometimes Jevon rushed the quarterback, sometimes he played the run, and sometimes he drifted into pass coverage. He made the SEC All-Freshman team and contributed 44 tackles and 2.5 sacks to the Florida defense.

The Gators lost only one game in 1996, a heartbreaker to rival Florida State. Still, the team's record was good enough to earn another shot at the national title. In a return match with Florida State in the Sugar Bowl that January, they dominated the Seminoles to finish the year as the top-ranked team in all of college football.

Although 1996 was a great year for Jevon as a football player, it brought still more tragedy to his family. That October, his brother Jermaine was standing on the street near the house when a car came by and a passenger opened fire. Jermaine was struck in the head and died. "It was the hardest thing I've ever gone through," says Jevon. "I'm still not over it. I think about him all the time."

Did You Know?

The most popular cards among Gator fans are still Emmitt Smiths'—Florida's greatest player.

Pure Power

chapter }

"If he wants, he can have an impact on every play in the game."

— FORMER FLORIDA DEFENSIVE
COORDINATOR BOB STOOPS

Head coach Steve Spurrier knew that Florida would not repeat its championship season in 1997. So many important players from the 1996 team had graduated that it was almost like starting from scratch. He also knew that the team's fortunes would depend on young players like Jevon Kearse, who had not been full-time starters. Spurrier's faith was rewarded when the Gators finished with a 10–2 record. The season ended on a high note when Florida beat Penn State in the Citrus Bowl to finish the year ranked fourth in the nation.

Jevon played very well in 1997, despite the fact that he started only three games. Bob Stoops decided the best way to use him was to continue "spotting" him at different positions in different situations. So although Jevon was technically a substitute, he

*Jevon (42) leads the way as teammate Cameron Davis
returns a fumble for a touchdown.*

Coach Spurrier was very satisfied with Florida's #4 ranking in 1997.

was on the field and in the middle of the action on every big play. After the season, he was voted All-SEC for his great performance.

As the Gators prepared for the 1998 season, Jevon started thinking about playing in the NFL. He knew that one more good year would be enough to make him a first-round draft pick (and a millionaire), and that would mean relief for his family. It pained Jevon to see his mother struggle, and Jermaine's death convinced him that he needed to do something soon before another sibling was taken by the streets.

One of the things that bothered Jevon was that he was not compensated for playing college football. The university made millions of dollars every time he stepped on the field, and yet his family still lived in poverty. In return for playing, Jevon received a few dollars to cover his basic expenses, and of course a free education. He valued the opportunity to learn (which many players squander) and he took summer classes so he could get his sociology degree early, but he still did not think he was getting a fair deal.

These feelings made Jevon a perfect target for Tank Black, a sports agent who befriended college athletes with the intention of representing them once they turned professional. This is against the rules, and every college athlete knows it. Still, Black had "understandings" with many young stars, who secretly accepted cash and presents from him. When Black offered to cover Lessie Mae's bills until Jevon made it to the NFL, he agreed to the arrangement. "I probably wouldn't do it again," says Jevon. "But

Agent Tank Black, who had an "understanding" with Jevon in college

then again…Tank was paying the bills and keeping money in my pocket."

Black's "investment" began paying dividends during the summer of 1998, when *The Sporting News* ran a three-page feature on Jevon, calling him the best linebacker in college football. A few weeks later, *ESPN The Magazine* profiled him and had more good things to say about his game. Jevon was the centerpiece of a killer defensive unit—one that some experts claimed was strong enough to take Florida back to the national championship game. He was joined by tackles Ed Chester and Reggie McGrew and fellow linebackers Mike Peterson and Johnny Rutledge. The Gators' season would hinge on its offense, which had a lot of question marks. Jesse Palmer and Doug Johnson were fighting over the quarterback job, and the top running and receiving jobs were also up for grabs.

In the season's third game, against Tennessee, the offense failed to put enough points on the board. Despite Jevon's heroics on defense, the Volunteers stunned the Gators 20–17, dimming their hopes of a national title.

Florida stayed in contention by winning its next seven games, and Jevon played like a whirlwind. When asked to start a game against Kentucky at defensive end, he responded with nine tackles. If the Gators could beat Florida State in the last regular season game, they would

Did You Know?

When Jevon starts running out of gas late in games, he uses Jermaine's death to motivate him. "Sometimes I imagine that the person who shot my brother might be the guy lined up across from me. If I'm feeling tired, I'm not tired anymore. My brother took two bullets to the head. No way I'm going to let being tired stop me."

"I feel like I've got a chance to make a play no matter where it is. It's all about my mode of thinking, just never being satisfied."

JEVON KEARSE

still get a shot at the championship. Unfortunately for Jevon and his teammates, their season stalled when the offense faltered once again. Florida lost, 23–12. In the season-ending Orange Bowl, Jevon played well against Syracuse in a 31–10 loss. It was to be his final college game.

That spring, Jevon decided to skip his final college season and make himself available in the NFL Draft. He had nothing left to prove at Florida, on or off the field. Jevon made All-SEC again and was named to several All-America teams. He also was a finalist for several major awards, including Defensive Player of the Year. In his mind, he had accomplished the four goals he had set for himself when he went to Gainesville: "To become a better person, to win a national championship, to get an education, and finally to have a chance to play in the NFL."

college *highlights*

SEC All-Freshman	1996
National Champion	1996
16.5 Career Sacks	1996–1998
All-SEC	1997, 1998
Butkus Award Finalist	1998
All-American	1998
Football News Defensive Player of the Year	1998

Jevon's Greatest
HITS

Long before Jevon pulled on a Tennessee Titans uniform, he was a giant on the football field. Here are some of his best college performances:

- 5 TACKLES, 2 SACKS, 2 FORCED FUMBLES VS. NORTHEAST LOUISIANA (1998)
- 7 TACKLES, 2.5 SACKS VS. ALABAMA (1998)
- 9 TACKLES, 1 INTERCEPTION VS. KENTUCKY (1998)
- 12 TACKLES VS. GEORGIA (1997)
- 9 TACKLES VS. FLORIDA STATE (1997)
- 9 TACKLES, 1 FORCED FUMBLE VS. GEORGIA SOUTHERN (1996)
- 8 TACKLES VS. KENTUCKY (1996)

Sweet Sixteen

"We think Jevon is special. In fact, we're going to put a lot of pressure on him from here on in to be special."

— TITANS' GM FLOYD REESE

As the 1999 NFL Draft neared, everyone agreed that Jevon Kearse was one of the most remarkable physical specimens to come out of college in years. In the February scouting combines, he recorded the second-fastest time in history in the 10-yard dash—a measure of how quickly a player explodes off the line of scrimmage (Deion Sanders still holds the record). Few, however, could agree on which position would be right for Jevon as a pro.

The problem was that, in college, he had rarely played in the same spot from game to game. He was such a destructive force that Florida had simply used him where he could do the most damage. As a result, he was not experienced at any one position. Also, there was not enough game film of Jevon at any one position for scouts to accurately evaluate his strengths and weaknesses.

Most teams considered Jevon a "project." That was a nice way of saying that it might take years to harness his raw ability and find a place for him on the field. Sometimes players like this take to the NFL immediately and become stars. But more

Jevon talks to reporters after being selected by the Titans in the 1999 NFL Draft.

often, they become lost and confused, and begin to doubt themselves. Some scouts felt Jevon was a "Tweener"—someone whose size and skill put him in between a defensive end and a linebacker. Tweeners often end up as career substitutes, because they cannot meet the demands of a set position play after play after play.

Jevon *did* have certain things in his favor. He was obviously a very intelligent and motivated young man. He also was incredibly fast for someone his size. He had added 50 pounds (23 kg) of muscle during his college years, yet he was even quicker than when he had started.

The Tennessee Titans considered Jevon a perfect fit for their team. They had the sixteenth pick in the draft, and needed someone who could make things happen on defense. Jevon fit the bill perfectly. The Titans had an aggressive, hard-hitting unit that lacked only one thing: someone who could crash into enemy backfields and pressure the quarterback. The Titans caused just 11 fumbles in 1998 and had a league-low 30 sacks. They drafted Jevon and told him it would be his job to turn those numbers around.

Many Tennessee fans questioned their team's pick. They blamed the Titans' 8–8 record on the *offense*, not the defense. Quarterback Steve McNair was still struggling to prove himself, running back Eddie George was used too much, and the team's receivers seemed either too slow, too old, or too injured to make clutch catches. Why, fans wondered, hadn't the club used its pick for a receiver or another runner?

Coach Jeff Fisher and general manager Floyd Reese believed the offense was just fine. It was certainly good enough to score two or three touchdowns a game, and with

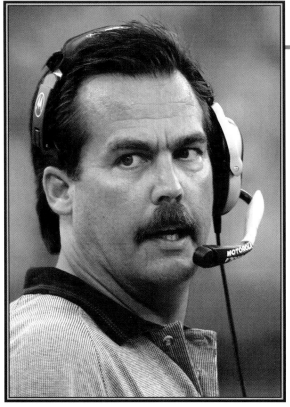

Tennessee Titans
head coach Jeff Fisher

a dominant defense, that was all the Titans would need to win. Too many times in 1998, opposing teams had burned Tennessee with long passing plays. Fisher and Reese believed that this was because they were given too much time to throw the ball. If Jevon could hurry passers into bad decisions, the team's talented cornerbacks, safeties, and linebackers could lay in wait for a wobbly pass and intercept it.

For his part, Jevon was ready to do whatever the Titans asked. He was insulted that he had not been selected sooner, and wanted to make the rest of the league pay for its mistake. "Fifteen teams passed me," he says. "I felt like I was one of the best people in the draft. The fact that I didn't go until sixteenth really motivated me."

On the first day of training camp, Jevon joined the rest of the team for the various tests NFL players go through before starting a season. He was poked, prodded, measured, weighed, and evaluated in every conceivable way. While waiting in line to have his vertical leap measured, Jevon asked Jerry Gray, who coached the defensive backs, whether he could skip the test if he could touch the ceiling. Gray looked up at the 12-foot (3.6-m) ceiling and smiled. "Sure," he said. Jevon took two steps, sprung into the air, and punched out a ceiling tile. He was excused.

The coaches taught Jevon the various defenses the Titans would use, and drilled him on how to deal with the blocking

Did You Know?

One of Jevon's first moves after the draft was to dump Tank Black. He no longer trusted the agent, and cut all ties to him. Other clients later accused Black of mishandling their money.

Nashville's Adelphia Coliseum, where Jevon played his first official NFL game

schemes he would encounter as a defensive end. They fed him information as fast as he could digest it. "They just put me at defensive end and worked with me," he remembers. "They were patient when I first went in, but they saw the potential. And that's when they really challenged me."

The 1999 season began in the Titans' new home, Adelphia Coliseum. The franchise had moved to Tennessee a few years earlier, after spending more than three decades playing as the Houston Oilers. The veterans told Jevon that while waiting for their stadium to be built, they had felt as if they were on the road 16 games a year. Adelphia certainly felt like home on this day, as a huge crowd cheered the Titans to a thrilling 36–35 win over the Cincinnati Bengals. Jevon held his own in his first pro game, despite being nervous at times.

The postgame celebration was cut short when word spread that McNair had injured his back and would require surgery. Luckily, the Titans had signed Neil O'Donnell to be McNair's backup. He was an experienced quarterback who had once led the Pittsburgh Steelers to the Super Bowl. During McNair's absence, O'Donnell played very well and the Titans won four of five games. It was during this time that Jevon became a major force.

In Tennessee's second game, against the Cleveland Browns, Jevon grabbed the spotlight when he destroyed Orlando Brown. Play after play, he overwhelmed the veteran tackle and completely disrupted the Cleveland offense. That evening, when the high-

Jevon kneels over quarterback Tim Couch after one of three sacks he got against the Browns in his second NFL game.

lights were aired on national television, it looked like the "Jevon Kearse Show," as his three sacks were replayed over and over again. The following week, Jevon wiped out the Jacksonville Jaguars with seven solo tackles as Tennessee's record improved to 3–0. The Jags were heavy favorites to win the American Football Conference (AFC) Central Division, where the Titans also happened to play. In all, the two clubs would meet three times during the 1999 season, and Jevon would play a major role in the outcome of each game.

The Titans lost to the San Francisco 49ers in Week 4, but once again Jevon was a dominant force. He was named NFL Defensive Rookie of the Month for September. Two victories followed, over the New Orleans Saints and the Baltimore Ravens. Neither team could handle Jevon, who was starting to look like a hands-down pick for Rookie of the Year.

With McNair back in the starting lineup for Week 7, the question was: *Are the 5–1 Titans for real?* The same question was being asked of their opponent, the St. Louis Rams, who had fashioned a 6–0 record after little-known Kurt Warner had replaced the injured starter, Trent Green. In this game, both teams definitely proved they were for real. They fought a tough battle, with neither giving in.

Did You Know?

In 1999, Jevon was in on at least one sack in each of the season's final nine games. He ran the string to 12 straight in 2000, establishing a new NFL record.

Early in the game, Jevon was the big difference. Rams' tackle Fred Miller simply could not handle him, and every time Warner got ready to pass, the Freak seemed to be in his face. In addition, Miller was whistled for six false-start penalties, which killed the St. Louis offense. Meanwhile, McNair helped the Titans build a 21–0 halftime lead. However, everyone in the stadium knew that lead was not secure.

Slowly but surely, the Rams regained control of the game. They either ran away from Jevon or assigned two blockers to deal with him. St. Louis matched Tennessee's three touchdowns in the second half, but the Titans held a 24–21 advantage on a field goal by Al Del Greco. In the game's final

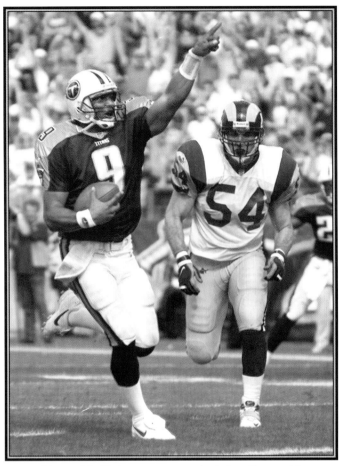

Steve McNair scores against the Rams. His running ability gives the Tennessee offense an added dimension.

seconds, the Rams drove to the 21-yard line and sent the field-goal unit in. Jeff Wilkins missed the kick as time expired, and the Titans escaped with a win. After the game, all anyone could talk about was Jevon's performance. Warner said the rookie was "relentless" and that what he had done to Miller was "unfair."

Tennessee won three of its next four games. During this time, Jevon took another important step forward. He had spent the entire summer learning how to play defensive end in the pros, and was now starting to master the position. The coaching staff realized that they had a special player on their hands, and began talking to Jevon about other ways they wanted to use him. Jevon was thinking right along with them. If he was

"I felt sorry for Fred [Miller]. I was thinking, 'We've got to do something to bail him out.'"

KURT WARNER, ON JEVON'S PERFORMANCE IN THEIR FIRST MEETING

the strongest defensive player on the field, why not line him up against the *weakest* part of an opponent's offense?

Now Jevon was the ultimate nightmare: a pass rusher who could beat any blocker in the league coming from a different angle on every play. The mayhem he caused led to sacks, interceptions, fumbles, and broken plays. The Titans did not just beat other teams; they demoralized them. And it pleased Jevon to know he was the cause of their misery. "I'm a selfish football player," he says. "Each time the ball is snapped, I tell myself that I want to make that tackle, make that big play."

Over the season's final five games, the Titans lost just once, to the Ravens. In that game, Jevon made one of the greatest defensive plays of all time. When the ball was snapped, he rushed passer Tony Banks, who was able to get a pass off to fleet-footed Qadry Ismail, who is nicknamed the Missile. Ismail eluded a couple of tacklers and then sprinted for the end zone with no one between himself and the goal line. He was probably counting the six points in his head when he was grabbed from behind and thrown to the ground like a rag doll. Ismail could hardly believe his eyes when he got up. The man who had caught him was Jevon Kearse.

After the game, all an embarrassed Ismail could do was joke about the play. "Jevon rushed the passer, stopped, sat down, took a drink of Gatorade on the sidelines, spoke to our coaches for a bit about why we didn't draft him," he smiled. "And then proceeded to run me down!"

The biggest game of the regular season took place against Jacksonville.

Did You Know?

Jeff Fisher's reputation for tough defense goes back to his days as a player. He was a standout defensive back at the University of Southern California and a member of the 1984 NFL champion Chicago Bears.

Although the Jaguars were ahead of the Titans in the division standings, Tennessee had enough wins to make the playoffs as a Wild Card. With his team on a roll, Coach Fisher was thinking about making it to the Super Bowl. He and the players knew this meant they would have to defeat Jacksonville in the postseason. Here was a great chance to "send a message" to the division leaders. The Titans delivered this message by destroying the Jags, 41–14.

Tennessee's final regular-season game came against the Pittsburgh Steelers—a team many picked to finish ahead of the Titans in 1999. In this game, Jevon completed what defensive players call the "Quadruple Crown" when he tackled quarterback Mike Tomczak. "I was able to get the sack, cause a fumble, recover the fumble, and take it in for six," he beams.

The play put an exclamation point on a year that saw Jevon cause a total of 10 fumbles and lead the AFC with 14.5 quarterback sacks, an NFL record for rookies. He also was named to the NFL All-Pro team, a rare accomplishment for a first-year player.

Jevon never doubted that he would make an impact in the NFL. But not even *he* could have imagined how successful he would be right from the start. A lot of the credit, he maintains, belongs to the Tennessee coaching staff. "In college I played linebacker," he says. "So for me to be able to come into the NFL and have the success I had, I owe everything to the coaches…they could have easily thrown a veteran out there and just waited until they molded me. But they had trust in me."

Quarterback Jay Fiedler crumbles under Jevon during Jacksonville's 41–14 loss to the Titans.

Road to the Super Bowl

chapter 5

"We know we can win with our defense."

— JEVON KEARSE

Tennessee's first playoff opponent was the Buffalo Bills. The Bills were very similar to the Titans. They had a tough defense that held opponents in check, and an offense that was good enough to put the ball in the end zone two or three times a game. Their Wild Card meeting was expected to be a tense battle that went down to the final play, and it did. Only the final play was perhaps the weirdest and wildest in postseason history.

"Sometimes I feel only I can stop myself."

JEVON KEARSE

Jevon wraps up Rob Johnson of the Bills to cause a safety in the 1999 Wild Card game.

Jevon was the story early in the contest, when he pounced on quarterback Rob Johnson in the end zone for a safety. After that, the Bills double- and triple-teamed Jevon on every play, which freed up his teammates to go after the ball. Meanwhile, Steve McNair and Eddie George led the Titans to a touchdown and a field goal, giving Tennessee a 12–0 lead. The Bills scored twice in the second half to take a 13–12 edge, but Al Del Greco booted a 36-yard field goal to put Tennessee out in front 15–13. On the game's final drive, Johnson marched the Bills down the field and Steve Christie kicked a field goal to retake the lead, 16–15, with just seconds remaining. All Buffalo had to do was kick-off and let time expire.

Eddie George completes a 68-yard touchdown run to give the Titans a 13–9 lead against the Colts in the playoffs.

This proved to be harder than the Bills thought. Christie grounded a low kick into the Tennessee return team. Lorenzo Neal shoveled the ball to tight end Frank Wycheck, who lumbered to his right with the entire Buffalo coverage team pursuing him. Suddenly, he whirled and lateraled across the field to receiver Kevin Dyson. The tackler assigned to guard this part of the field had slipped when Wycheck threw the ball, leaving Dyson a clear path to the end zone. The speedster scored easily to pull off the "Music City Miracle" and send the Titans to the second round of the playoffs.

There they met the Indianapolis Colts, led by the terrific trio of Peyton Manning, Edgerrin James, and Marvin Harrison. Jeff Fisher decided the best way to defend the Indy offense was to keep it off the field. The strategy was for McNair and George to control the ball and eat up the clock with long drives. The plan worked perfectly, as the Titans' offense wore down the Colts' defense, while the Titans' defense remained fresh. In the second half, George rumbled 68 yards for a touchdown to give Tennessee a 13–9 lead. Manning made a gallant comeback at the end, but the Colts fell short by a score of 19–16. Once again, the Titans

Did You Know?

When Jevon rushes the passer, he picks a spot on the field and decides that is where he will beat his man. He says that knowing when and where he will make his moves gives him the advantage. "If you pick a spot and beat a guy to that spot, it's over."

By the AFC title game, Jevon was 25 pounds lighter than when he started the season.

had prevailed in a tense defensive battle.

Now it was time to take on the Jaguars for the AFC title—and see just how important those first two wins really were. So far in the playoffs, Coach Fisher had asked his defensive unit to come up big twice in a row, and the strain was beginning to show. Several players were slowed by minor injuries, including Jevon. To put them in another low-scoring game might be asking too much. So rather than grinding out yards on battering-ram running plays, Fisher told McNair to open things up and "stretch" the Jaguars with an aggressive passing attack.

Unfortunately, Jacksonville was not surprised. They had been burned for five TD passes by McNair in their previous meeting, and suspected the Titans might try to blow them out again. The Jacksonville pass rush was strong, and the secondary made quality plays when it had to. At halftime, the Titans trailed 14–10. Some Tennessee players doubted whether it was worth continuing this plan. But McNair believed it would, and

Derrick Mason runs for daylight against the Jaguars. His touchdown return of a free kick guaranteed the Titans a trip to the Super Bowl.

so did Jevon. Both would play key roles in the second half.

The Titans scored immediately in the third quarter to take a 17–14 lead, and they never looked back. The key play came in the third quarter and, as usual, Jevon was right in the middle of it. The Jags, pinned deep in their own territory, called for a rollout pass. As quarterback Mark Brunell walked to the line of scrimmage, he saw that Jevon was lined up perfectly to stop the play.

Brunell called time-out, talked with his coaches, and the call was changed to a straight drop-back pass. When the ball was snapped, Jevon exploded past tackle Ben Coleman, which forced his old Florida teammate, Fred Taylor, to make an impossible choice: *Do I slide over and crash into Jevon, or stay put and help with the two Titans burrowing through the middle of the line?* Taylor flashed over to block Jevon, and an instant later Josh Evans and Jason Fisk pulled down Brunell for a safety.

Tennessee, ahead 19–14, received the free kick that follows a safety, and Derrick Mason returned it all the way for a touchdown that broke the game open. The final score was 33–14. The Tennessee Titans had a date with the St. Louis Rams in Super Bowl XXXIV!

Super Freak

"Oh, we'll be ready for him."

— JIM HANNIFAN, ST. LOUIS
OFFENSIVE LINE COACH

lthough happy to be headed to the Super Bowl, Jevon Kearse was a bruised and battered young man. He had dropped 25 pounds (11 kg) during the season, and it hurt just to get out of bed in the morning. Including exhibitions, he was about to play in his 24th game—twice the number he had played during a typical college season. Coach Fisher was worried that Jevon was wearing down. He also knew what the Rams were planning for the rookie.

The St. Louis coaches were watching the same game films Fisher was. They would see that, although the Tennessee defense had stopped the Jaguars cold, Jacksonville had found a way to stop Jevon. Their strategy was simple and brutal. Besides the straight-on blocking by Ben Coleman, another

Did You Know?

Jevon could one day become only the third player in franchise history to be named league MVP. Quarterback George Blanda won the award in 1961 and running back Earl Campbell took the trophy in 1979—both as Houston Oilers.

Isaac Bruce hauls in a pass early in Super Bowl XXXIV. He would keep the Tennessee defense busy all day.

Jacksonville player always took a shot at Jevon, especially when the referees were not looking. Although he still dominated within his area, he was rarely able to break out and get to the ball. As expected, the Rams decided to follow the same plan.

Jevon found it hard to recover his strength, even though he had two weeks off before the Super Bowl. Part of the problem was that he was one of the most in-demand

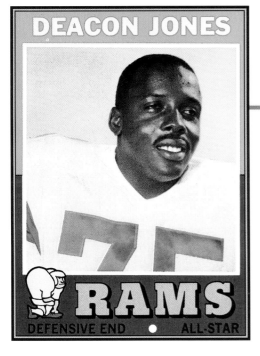

DEACON JONES

RAMS

DEFENSIVE END • ALL-STAR

Fans of "sack specialists" like Deacon Jones must now add Jevon's trading card to their collections. Says Jones: "He has the speed, the quickness, the desire—a will to get to the quarterback no matter where he is on the field. He wants to attack, attack, attack."

players by the media. The exhausted rookie had to do interview after interview, and could not go anywhere without a microphone or tape recorder being shoved in his face. It got so bad that the Titans actually had to limit access to Jevon so he could have a moment of peace and quiet.

As expected, Super Bowl XXXIV was a war. Tennessee's great defense held St. Louis's great offense to just nine points in the first half, but the Titans could not score at all against the Rams. Jevon was not 100 percent, but he *gave* 100 percent, forcing the Rams to go through with their plan. This created openings for Jevon's teammates, who made big tackles when the Titans most needed them.

In the third quarter, the Rams scored a touchdown to make the score 16–0. Steve McNair and Eddie George came right back, as they had so many times during the season, and scored two straight touchdowns to make the score 16–13. With just two minutes left, Al Del Greco booted a 43-yard field goal to knot the score at 16–16. The Titans kicked off and the Rams got ready to mount their final attack.

The Rams' first play from scrimmage will be replayed a thousand times. Super Bowls are won by great players making great plays, and in the span of a few seconds three extraordi-

Did You Know?

Jevon's explosive pass-rushing style reminds many of two NFL greats, Lawence Taylor and Derrick Thomas.

nary plays were made by three tremendous players. The ball was snapped, and Jevon mustered every last bit of energy in his tired body. He rolled right over a shocked Fred Miller and headed for quarterback Kurt Warner, who had taken an extra step on his

Jevon bats down a third-quarter pass by Kurt Warner. Jevon was in Warner's face all game, and came within an inch or two of preventing Warner's game-winning throw to Isaac Bruce.

drop back. Sensing he was in trouble, Warner rushed his throw. He barely completed his follow-through when Jevon's right arm clubbed him to the turf. Warner put just enough of an extra flick on the ball to get it near his receiver, Isaac Bruce, who adjusted in mid-stride to catch the under-thrown pass. Bruce then put a couple of Hall-of-Fame moves on the defensive backs and ran 73 yards for a touchdown.

Down but not out, the Titans got the ball with more than a minute left. As Jevon watched from the sideline, McNair engineered a magnificent drive all the way to the 10-yard line. With time left for one last play, McNair hit Kevin Dyson with a short pass over the middle. As he strained for the end zone, linebacker Robert Jones pulled him down just a few feet short of the goal line as time expired on the most thrilling Super Bowl in history. Tennessee had lost 23–16, but there was nothing to be ashamed of.

After the game, Jevon was not ashamed. He was *furious*. He knew he had made a great play, and still could not believe that the Rams had scored. Jevon announced that Warner was lucky and that the Titans were the better team. Normally, reporters chalk up such remarks to poor sportsmanship. But in Jevon's case, they knew it was a great young player going through his first heartbreaking loss. They could have roasted him for it. Instead, they chose not to make a big deal out of it. That is the kind of respect players hope for, but rarely get. After just one season, Jevon had established himself as a true professional.

Kevin Dyson stretches in vain as time runs out for the Titans in Super Bowl XXXIV.

Keep Moving Forward

chapter 7

"Now I see a lot of respect. Quarterbacks are looking for me."
— JEVON KEARSE

A week after the Super Bowl, Jevon showed up for the Pro Bowl in Hawaii. He was back to his fun-loving, hardworking self again. In fact, he was so upbeat that the other players had to ask him to cool it. He was so pumped in practice that they were afraid the coaches would expect *them* to work that hard. Jevon could not help it. Getting a chance to play in the NFL's all-star game had long been a dream of his.

As luck would have it, on the game's first series, Jevon found himself going after Kurt Warner again. Warner unloaded a long pass that was caught by Randy Moss for a 48-yard gain. *Here we go again!* thought Jevon. The NFC triumphed 51–31, but this loss did not hurt very much. The game was mostly for fun.

Did You Know?

Jevon was the first AFC rookie ever to make All-Pro at defensive end.

Jevon's warm manner and big smile make him one of pro football's most popular players.

While in Hawaii, Jevon finally started to understand what a special year he had had. "I started out fast, and it was all desire and wanting to show people there was no way I should have been drafted that low," he says. "When I got to the Pro Bowl and realized there were only three other defensive ends on the AFC team, that was when I realized what I had accomplished."

After returning to Florida, Jevon had a lot more time to look back over his tremendous rookie season. He was a unanimous choice for NFL Defensive Rookie of the Year,

Jevon cannot believe he has just been named 1999 Defensive Rookie of the Year.

and was Defensive Rookie of the Month in every month except October. Jevon was also named NFL Defensive Player of the Month for December. Many were calling him the best young pass rusher in history. Is he? Jevon is no historian, but he does recognize that he brings something special to the job. He also thinks he can get a lot better.

"I feel like I've helped create a new standard of hustle for defensive linemen," he says. "Now I want to do twice as much as I've been doing. Six or seven years from now someone bigger, stronger, and faster will come along and they'll call him the new *improved* Freak. Until then I need to raise the bar as high as I can."

Jevon knew he would face a lot more resistance in his second year. Everyone had a year's worth of film on him. But then *he* had a year's worth of experience under his belt. "Seeing all the double-teams and triple-teams and all the different shifting to try to mess my head up—it really prepared me," he says.

Did You Know?

The only other Tennessee Pro Bowl starter in 1999 was center Bruce Matthews, the oldest player on the team.

It did indeed. During the 2000 season, most teams went into their games against the Titans with one major goal: Don't get "Freaked out." Often they doubled up on Jevon with a tackle and tight end. Sometimes they used a guard and a tackle. Jevon's sack opportunities and tackles went down, but the Tennessee defense continued to produce one bone-crushing win after another. As defensive coordinator Gregg Williams and others were quick to point out, all of the attention lavished on Jevon early in 2000 just made it easier to execute the team's defensive game plan. As long as opponents were satisfied tying up two players on Jevon, then other players like Kenny Holmes were free to come in and finish off plays.

By mid-season, however, this strategy was beginning to take its toll on Jevon. Proud and powerful, he fought the double-teams with all his might. He fought so hard, in fact, that team doctors had to start giving him intravenous fluids between halves. Jevon was getting so exhausted that at one point opponents were able to get away with single-man blocking. Often, Jevon would lose his concentration looking around for an imaginary second blocker. And all the while, he was fighting a painful hip injury. In short, he was learning what it took to be a star in the NFL.

The biggest difference between his first and second season? "Expectations," Jevon says. "I guess everyone pretty much expects me to get two, three sacks a game." According to Jevon, another difference was that officials were no longer throwing their flags whenever he was held illegally by offensive linemen. Sometimes they just turned the other way.

The bright side of Jevon's 2000 season was that the Titans were winning and he was continuing to learn about his position. He was recognizing plays faster and getting to the right spot quicker, which had a positive effect on the entire team. Still, Jevon felt that his lack of sacks meant he was getting worse, not better. Coach Williams sat him down and told him he had nothing to fear. He was actually grading out higher than the year before, making far fewer rookie mistakes. And, said Williams, he was "light-years

EXCLUSIVE: TOP 40 SACKERS OF ALL TIME

NFL INSIDER

JEVON!
TITANS' KEARSE LEADS A NEW BREED OF PASS RUSHERS

PLUS
SHANNON SHARPE · STEVE McNAIR
KEVIN CARTER · LAWRENCE TAYLOR

LIFE IN THE ARENA LEAGUE

NOVEMBER 2000

$3.99 USA · $4.99 CAN
WWW.NFL.COM

pro *highlights*

NFL Defensive Rookie of the Year	1999
NFL All-Pro	1999
AFC Champion	1999
Pro Bowl Selection	1999, 2000
10+ Sacks	1999, 2000

ahead on his understanding and feel for the game." That made Jevon feel better.

So did the three sacks he got in Week 10 against the Ravens. By early December, Jevon was back to his old self, leading the Titans in tackles and sacks, and finding new ways to create havoc at the line of scrimmage. The league had adjusted to him, and he had adjusted to the adjustment. Jevon was starting to do the thing the team wanted most: add his tremendous intelligence to his eye-popping athletic ability.

The Titans finished the 2000 season with the NFL's best record. Jevon ended up with 10.5 sacks, giving him the second-highest total (25) for a player in his second year. Heading into the playoffs, the Titans feared only one team, the trash-talking Baltimore Ravens. Their defense was even stingier than Tennessee's, and they had a great special-teams unit. In their two regular-season games, Tennessee had won 14–6 in a defensive battle, then lost 24–23 when Al Del Greco missed an extra point and a field goal.

Jevon and his teammates watched Baltimore beat the Denver Broncos in the Wild Card game. As they prepared for their meeting with the Ravens, they knew there were two things they could not afford to do: miss kicks and commit turnovers. The Ravens' plan was to keep Tennessee's blockers busy with their big front line so that linebacker Ray Lewis—the NFL's Defensive Player of the Year—could roam free and cause havoc.

As expected, the game turned into a defensive war. Jevon and company kept the Ravens bottled up all day, limiting quarterback Trent Dilfer to 5 completions and 1,000-yard rusher Jamal Lewis to a mere 47 yards. But Lewis was all over the field for Baltimore, making 12 tackles to shut down George and McNair.

As Jevon feared, the game turned on kicks and turnovers. Del Greco missed three of four field goals. Two of his attempts were deflected, with one being run all the way back for a touchdown that broke a 10–10 tie in the third quarter. With the Titans

You don't get much hotter than Jevon. Not even a slow start in 2000 could keep him off the cover of the NFL's official magazine.

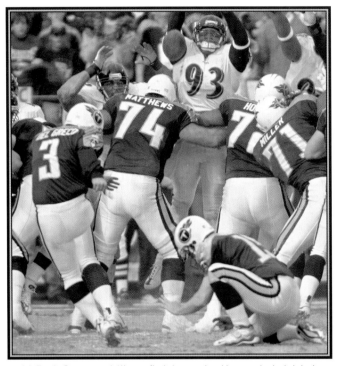

Al Del Greco drills a field goal attempt right into the waiting arms of the Baltimore Ravens. In his four tries, the Titans scored just three points... while the Ravens scored six!

driving late in the game for a game-tying score, disaster struck when George bobbled a short pass. Lewis snatched it away from him and took it in for a touchdown to make the final score 24–10. The Ravens went on to beat the Oakland Raiders in the AFC championship game, then defeated the New York Giants in the Super Bowl. As Jevon watched the games, he could not help thinking that it should have been the Titans playing for the trophy again.

The unexpected loss to the Ravens was not the first setback Jevon has suffered, nor will it be the last. He has been through too much in his young life to think he's got it made, regardless of how much he achieves. Yet Jevon has also come far enough to understand that—if you look hard enough—there is bound to be a little bit of good in everything, no matter how bad it seems.

He even sees something positive in the death of his father, a man he never got a chance to meet—a man with whom, he has slowly learned, he shares more than a last name. "If I had grown up with a father, maybe I wouldn't have pushed myself to where I am right now," offers Jevon. "Maybe I wouldn't need to play football, because my mom and dad would have jobs. By not having a father—and wanting to help my family be financially stable—that's motivated me to be the kind of person, and player, I am today.

"Everything I've gone through," insists Jevon, "has made me strong."

Jevon is now an old pro with the media. Here he runs his own impromptu press conference.

Index